Between

Amelia Díaz Ettinger

Early Praise for *Between*

❖

What a pleasure to watch the poems of Amelia Díaz Ettinger deepen with close observation and clarity over time. Her latest collection, *Between*, shows us a poet unafraid to become one with the land she has come to both love and respect, each new poem offering us "an unexpected plenitude/not of ruin/but solace."

—JAMES CREWS, author of *Turning Toward Grief*
and *Breathing Room*

❖

In *Between*, Amelia Díaz Ettinger invites us into the nuanced layers between solitude and connection, between silence and the call of an owl, between what we were taught and what we know, between our past and our present. These poems are filled with both ferocity and gratefulness, each one an invitation to "get close and see" what is here—sometimes beautiful, sometimes unwanted. I admire her precision, her attentiveness, her curiosity as she explores motherhood, citizenship, the body, language, and the natural world. These are poems that both ground us in what is here and reach toward what else might be possible.

—ROSEMERRY WAHTOLA TROMMER, author of *The Unfolding*
and host of The Poetic Path

REDBAT BOOKS
PACIFIC NORTHWEST
WRITERS SERIES

BETWEEN

— POETRY BY —

AMELIA DÍAZ ETTINGER

REDBAT BOOKS
LA GRANDE, OREGON
2025

Printed in the United States of America

First Edition: October 2025

Trade Paperback ISBN: 978-1-946970-05-3
    Library of Congress Control Number: 2025945783

Published by
redbat books
La Grande, OR 97850
www.redbatbooks.com

Text set in Alegreya

Cover painting:
"Wander" *by* Craig Appleby

Book design by
Kristin Summers, redbat design | www.redbatdesign.com

Table of Contents

II
Between Blood and Skin—*because turmoil arises between layers*

III
Between the Legacies of Memory——*because there is always a beginning to the eye of the lizard*

*The best dreams are caught in early morning
with the spindly-crystal net of eagerness
between the eye of the lizard and the moon.*

I

Between Layers
—because the present manifests itself

The Deer Woman

Soon the valley will be full of snow,
and light from a sun doesn't burn,

doesn't bite. A light that enters
with this calm will dizzy me.

I look through the wet windows
they are stained with liquid sequins.

No sound penetrates this gray,
my heart understands this quiet rhythm.

It is the light of November
augury of shadow, winds of snow,

of stale kisses that taste of bitter coffee.
A silent doe searches tender buds in the dullness,

her tremulous steps whisper
the marvel of her round bones under her matted coat.

This light calms her and alerts her.
Orphan light,

the light of deer,
of woman,

of calmness,
and eventually of ruin.

Forbidding Meadow

is covered with a dusting of snow.
Like a Bundt cake with powdered sugar

a deceiving invitation to enter.
Discarded fences covered in lichen,

rusted old barbwire hidden among the dry,
weeds along with slats of wood turned to sand.

— "Trespassing prohibited"
— "Violators will be shot"

My neighbors boast this savage
language, and I look at the trees for clemency.

These firs and ponderosas are the sentinels,
portentous guardians set in periphery.

What language would they use?
Would they prosecute?

They are not immune to violence
last summer their screams drowned

under the arthropod arms of a tree
shear, few remain here on this spot.

Near the sign, a stump lies where the fence has fainted low,
even the mighty can be cut, now a seat—

to rest and evoke
how high these trees once reached.

as I wait
a snowflake lands

Winter Solstice

the stores on Main are dressed with Christmas kitsch
families shopping to the cadence of a Salvation Army bell

all wearing light coats and few scarves
no snow this year,

this lack, this negligence of nature,
almost makes me glad.

The lack of snow makes me feel I've scored a point
against all the merriment that I can't feel.

But the meanness of that thought shames me

there are no papier-mâché
statues of the Three Kings
larger than life
dressed with colorful silks that float with the ocean winds
near El Morro fortress, now a dream
there are no relatives
pinning for a shot of coquito with an excess of rum
nor neighbors bringing tembleque or pasteles de lechón
with a villancico de "Abremé la Puerta..."

no,

there are only semi-crowded streets in this small Eastern
     Oregon town—
where I made the choice to live.

I recognize familiar faces passing by,
holding smiles for their people, they have come home.

I am going to a house that has a tree
cut from the woods beyond my meadow, a tree with
few decorations

quiet conversation,
but alas,

I celebrate
there is very little snow.

A Drive in the Blues,
a Blizzard

stops everything, white light—
survives.

Color, sound, and breath
thrown onto the same altar.

Quiet suspended by a string,
a necklace of frost,

holds the flame of a warm body
searching respite.

Finds in whiteness
an unexpected plenitude

not of ruin
but solace.

Winter's Vise Grip

holds stern
the Grand Ronde valley.

These snow clouds in April
graying an impassive sky

slows the tender sprouts
in gardens.

In last year's compost
a small insolent asparagus

fires its florid purple finger
to firmament

as if to say,
you cannot frighten me.

Tracks on the Snow at Highway 204

I followed a wolf's trail in this early snow
I paused where he paused,

turned as he turned.
A stalker on thin skis.

A print firm, a single line
a necklace in diamond white,

a footprint is a reverse step,
but here the reverse is reverential.

I could feel his eyes and taste his moves
teasing me further into these woods.

I lost his trail once and found I had gone
in circles, *touché*, I thought with a smile.

Here were the ghostly screams of
a snowshoe hare, quick saunter from solace.

By a tree well,
I sat and watched.

The filigree lace left by a tiny mouse,
such a quiet yet eloquent mark.

I grabbed my poles and wished my tracks
were not these long graceless scars.

Trail to Black Lake

is steep, torturous, and charmed.
On the top there is room for a waltz.

"One two three, one two three."

A tree counts the measure,
the song, of course, the wind.

On this trek you dance on skinny skis,
with luck you are alone to surrender.

In this masquerade ball, the Douglas firs come dressed
with thick coats, they step aside

as bishops, mermaids, altar boys in diamond white,
their invitation; *Dance, dance, dream in winter.*

At this eminence you kiss a passing cloud,
the sun over Gunsight becomes your child,

(this being the true wizard).
Withered wombs open to the cold.

Only the gray jay, the robber
swoops down

to steal away
even you.

Descendants of Grande Ronde
During This Time of Change

On the way to town,
the grass fields harvested,

discover an ocean of sheep
covering the stubble of cut wheat.

The sheep is nitrogen and phosphor—
a new treaty for the soil.

This farmer no longer bound
to chain agronomy, or burning fields.

Sheep, soil, and charm
blooms again in the valley.

The pronghorns and the coyote
return, but the elk retreats.

Not a bucolic landscape, mind,
but a sign of these times.

In the fatigue of summer
the air still chokes with ash.

Splendor of Hidden Roots

Why do trees conceal
the splendor of their roots?
—PABLO NERUDA, *The Book of Questions*

Why indeed?
When they are the living mountains,

hidden,
under all these up and down hills.

All through each season, these mountain roots,
dressed in perpetual night, speak

a chemical language of precision
older than the earth at dusk.

In this darkness, communion
is given by twisted hairy tubes, a neighborhood,

a nervous system composed of mushrooms.
A humble web that counsels

exhilaration and alert,
at times celebration.

They know every leaf that fell.
If it was ravished, foe or savior.

These hybrid roots scream
and whisper gossip.

Above, the tree might sing
sharing song with wind.

The foliage will devour a ray sun,
the essential chain.

But below, away from prying eyes,
lies courage and community.

Visited by blind
careful weavers

small servants in the eternal night
who bear witness to the splendor.

Given eyes, would they marvel
at those mountains above?

Larix laricina's **Vision**

My tamarack does not curve, she bruises the sky
with straight and unwavering touch, sharp

as a splinter in the eye of the cloud, she cuts.
At his height the sky whispers, she listens,

the braggart recounting his past fury
from inglorious gray to white ruin.

She relinquishes no secrets,
exposes her delicate branches, a disarray

of eyelashes. A common harlot below lays
her robes. A surprise cover for rocks and lichen

under the appreciative eye of the sun,
a yellow that is his own relation.

My tamarack talks with a flicker,
a growing family inside her watchful eye.

Tough skin alive with extravagant percussion,
a generosity, a nurturing to a tyrant.

This warm rendition of her nobility to cloud, bird, and sun.
Under her flaking leather bark there is blood.

Umatilla's Nine Mile Trail

In summer your step is dust.
Soil turned to crushing sand.

Flies, moths, and the occasional biker
appear as a testament of summer.

They fracture the silence of a relentless sun,
even birds fly quiet in this heat.

In the canyon, at a distance, the smoke,
wildfires, and ruined lives.

Haze obfuscates the patchwork of farms
rendering beauty mute.

A random quilt blurred gray
among grotesque white arms—the new windmills.

The sweet aroma of skunk cabbage
and impossibly dry earth—they pray for summer's rain.

A lightness brought forth by paper-thin skeletons
desiccated shadows of yesterday's flowers.

In the shade, the sweet current of air as a river
brings absolution to the perceived scorching solitude.

Then, a sudden crushing branch—
reminder we share the dust.

Rings Upon Rings
Aquarius remigis

as if a torrent of rain
wants to drown this pond—

Get close and see.

These ripples, not of rain,
but water skippers!

A city on legs
balanced on the skin of water.

In a game, or maybe a war,
of meet and retreat.

The smaller ones race
for a brief connection,

in a second secrets shared
new circles inflate, shimmer

and fracture the calm
of a cloudy day

distort the mirror of trees
a vibration of branches

making the summer dance,
this is the hallucinogenic power

of walking on water.

Seven Poles Circled Chief Joseph's Dreams

We did not know the history of this place
at the top of the curve, on the Minam Pass.

We used to stop or slow the car
a ritual to watch honeybees

swarming on red basalt.
An unnerving need to pause

not knowing we were showing our respect
by pausing for the ghost of seven poles.

At first it was just him and me.
The children joined the ceremony years later,

making the climb in the safety
of our car, claiming this territory,

their glee at those small bodies seen then unseen
in bright sunlight. My son called it the Yellow Dance.

Mesmerized by the living spectrum
movement and distant buzz of time,

then I wondered if the rocks tasted of honey;
now I wonder if the honey was heavy with rocks.

Gentiana, Trumpet Shaped Flowers
Announce Spring in Mount Emily

Small things give me comfort
like finding a patch of Gentian

in a sea of grass and leaves.
Their blue-violet intensity

with round mouths almost black
and a target dot of yellow.

Are they mocking the sameness
around them, all that luscious green?

So many of these flowers
here on top of Mount Emily.

Eruptions of purple, an early gift
from torrential rains that flooded the valley.

Rains that made mud rivers in the streets
they kept me indoors for so long.

But here they are here with me
sharing a bit of sunshine and simplicity.

Small things give me comfort.

Conflagrations Abound

A gray gossamer of smoke
covers the Grande Ronde valley.

Air thick as stone,
the suffocating tongue of summer.

Elkhorns and Wallowa hide
under an airless curtain of carbon.

Birds, sound, and color
obliterated by man's folly.

Airways coated with the taste
of loss, disintegration.

Particles of firs, furs, and dreams
ablaze in those distant tornado fires.

The abundant yellow-jackets bite
oblivious in this change of climate.

Nehalem Bay, Oregon

the tang of salt and fish
on this briny bay's thin wake

breaks the boundary
of a hung sky over liquid

overturned by the sudden
turbulence of a motor boat

grayness spreading
in thin buffered layers—

an undulating mirror
where a translucent medusa

floats unaware

Old Formation

Moss grows like marble
in this random room I sleep,

ever dropping drops of dew
covering the green seen only in a desert

free-falling to this abyss of solitude
Hold tight!

For it is frail,
the life we make, where we lay

firm without foundation
green droplets on the abyss.

(following the form of a Mary Ruffle poem)

Pour Green Tea,

add a quarter teaspoon
of ginger and turmeric

a pinch of black pepper,
and a whole lot of honey.

The best dreams are caught in early morning
between the eye of the lizard and the moon.

But isn't honey the color of sunset, "el ocaso"?
Even midday fills with dread.

"El ocaso de la vida" rings,
turns desirable flesh to empty husk.

Force an image of morning!
Lead back to center!

Celebrate! Not just honey,
local honey,

Oregon's honey, Imbler's honey
to be precise.

Inevitably

Autumn returns,
with a coat of vermilion that falls.

Old aches awaken in
fainting leaves.

Autumn is best seen with no eyes,
hands in gardener's gloves.

Want to contain the exodus,
hope to find a single summer leaf.

Maybe a leaf shaped as a sword,
entangled in a filigreed spider's web.

That might halt an early snow,
a leaf of transubstantiation.

Could we plant a leaf like that,
hope to harvest it in early winter?

Raise it to the dying skies,
before it also turns to rust?

For now, it is Autumn,
and smoke flourishes at Mount Emily's lap.

Rakes scratch at morning frost—
the gardener sighs and hears a hunter's solitary shot.

but our earth is flat

and we have reached this edge
we have no ropes

nothing to hold on
or rivers to drown in

our life is full

of hidden rocks
we step we falter

and sometimes
yes

we hope

II

Between Blood and Skin
—because turmoil arises between layers

The Lies I Tell:

I am a slow reader
and words take a pause

under this fat Ponderosa
each letter leaps and disappears

I realized I have read that line twice,
twice over, it makes a dust devil

gathering strength in a frenzied dance.
Higher, past the firs,

senseless sentences whisper
old names, blurred edges.

Put that book down after all these years
alone at last with hiking sticks

I feel the dirt gather
in that place between my breasts.

Sit on a rock, granite
a sole protector within these well-known woods,

I wonder where it came from, the top of the mountain?
Is not what it seems.

Familiarity Breeds Invisibility

not to rob the tanager's orange-yellow surprise—
after all, he brings the happiness of a ripe apple in early June—

nor to steal the enthusiasm of warblers—
yellow, green, and gray, flirting about a bush with gabbled song—

or the marvel of a condor's wide span, which carries the whole sky—
with the mastery of all birds of prey—

Binoculars seldom scan for the ubiquitous house sparrow,
that late comer, or even spy a meadowlark.

Yet, a garden robin offers her nest.
Humble ofrenda that says, "Blue to rest memory."

Consider the junco's small brown body,
her darkest eyes, our own familiarity,

her panic flights full of toil,
her outer tail feathers, two long white banners.

It is the junco in the quiet of winter snow
who moves landscape, brings a bit of warmth.

to sit by the window

until the body is left behind
no longer a hindrance

of pain and sinew
but a blend of landscapes

some very distant
some so close at hand

here there are no heart beats
no inhalations

just air
soil and light

even total darkness
with the intensity of a clear sky

or ephemeral
like that cloud over there

The Causal Loop

Why does the twilight fade
sentiment and arrogance

onto a sweet, not quite forgotten,
lullaby?

Time marks your presence.
Shadow in your passing, reflected

upon flesh, marrow, and tune.
It fills the nightly owl

its strange and haunting call.
It turns hunger into song

and song into memories.
These too vanish by volition

not quite like fog.
Trails are avoided no more

now in search of a languid journey,
a passage of steel and stealth.

No heroic landscapes to form a circle,
just the quiet repose

of oceans panting with foam
sand burnished by abandonment.

Time at the still center.

The Road Curves

before you reach the pond
full of pintails and reeds.

There is an American flag—
in tatters.

Fringes flap like tentacles,
an octopus that makes drivers

slow and sough.
This flag stands in rich soil,

maybe the wealthiest in our county
yet the farmer seems surrendered.

The wind here can be fierce,
but maybe it is the wind of the day,

because sometimes
it feels hard to breathe.

Rubber Necks Make News

a murder of magpies descends
on a skunk carcass

by the side of the road.
An odd frenzy in black and white.

Black beaks pick and pull
drunk with the discovery,

tendons, hair, and dirt split and torn—
a few pecks at one another.

A misshapen magpie gets too close
a harsh caw and a strike land fiercely on his side.

The outcast hops
a bloody retreat.

The ruckus has alerted
masses of birds to join the spectacle.

Telephone lines bounce
with crows and cowbirds.

Their hunger averted by voyeurism
a discordant cacophony.

For even here, news like this,
this news travels fast.

Cycle

Memory alters
infinite firmaments.

Changes go on
making us stumble

on wide open paths
with the essence of a tumbleweed—

a canvas; an ecru sea of sandstones.
Imagine finding horses here,

storms,
and rusted feathers.

Even riders sleeping,
hands outstretched, reaching

for stars that fall
onto black pools.

So It Seems

to have come to this:
two layers of color trapped

between an unraveling banner
as frail and tender

as your thoughts and mine
producing fear of invaders

merely rumored yet
drift as cumulus

in our own unforgiving sky
where no beam is a port

and no port leads to safety

Calliope in This Millennium

sits alone or with her sisters.
They sigh and knit each other's hair.

Though they touch and prod them
for centuries, those below have turned to cattle.

This recent age of vulgarity has left them breathless
though some still stand strong forever growing

smaller celebrations—
Melpomene excluded; she understands better than most.

The cattle now confuse
beauty for violence, waste for eloquence.

She shifts her posture on the verge of defeat,
wants a surrender, ageless tranquility.

She wants to transform their bovine ways
with golden threads and honey air.

But their eyes are now opaque,
they forget the treasures of ages.

This error from an unforeseen mutation:
a loss that could endanger even goddesses.

Dear Señor Neruda, Because:

I want to follow your conflagrant ink,
your invocation to destroy Nixon.

My fingers cruise the Body Electric.
Again a blood-patriarch headquarters

germ words without decorum from his throne.
A woman's body is no longer sacred.

Show me how to find autonomous rhyme
'Dull-faced immigrant' carries a face of fear.

Now Only the 'well-off' laze in safety
under her seven spikes and torch obscured.

Dear Bard, unlike you, I can't write his name
I want to give no credence to this man.

Tell the 'gray hand' that no one belongs here
no longer a place in this procession.

―――――

Cominezo a Invocar a Walt Whitman by PABLO NERUDA
I Sing the Body Electric by WALT WHITMAN

Ruckle Road Quarantine

My street is always deserted, that's nothing new
what is empty is my table; too early for flowers
too dangerous for friends.

Yet, my kitchen, this sanctuary where I linger
to find my flavor of quiet solitude brims
with the aroma of yeast and honey.

I turn the sticky dough and it clings to my fingers
warm and familiar, so much like the skin
of the grandkids I long to touch.

Soon my kitchen will brim with English muffins
that I will freeze for a time when flowers
bloom, and wine will flow again in company

Out of Paradise

A Solano flower posing
on top of its blade of grass
can feel the warm dust
of a freeway at high traffic

People walking on concrete
can't hear the gentle cracking
of a spruce-fir moss spider
or see the Palos Verdes blue
caught in the light of Red Pine bark

Too many layers separate us
    a supermarket parking lot
    carts full of plastic bags
    an ocean of hunger
away from the crystal veins
on a Hine's emerald dragonfly
or the watery ball
of a Pacific Northwest truffle
fruiting body against loud conversations
television forfeits
the murmur of trees at dusk

Layers of separation hide stars at night
the computer screen light blinds
the loneliness of a mussel
on a rock at low tide

the Sumatran Rhino died
but the klaxon horns intensified

we cannot   stop

we can't mourn what we can't see
too many layers we layer
ourselves out of paradise

At a Writer's Workshop
Summer of '18, Joseph, Oregon

We sat in a half circle, surrounded by night,
nature, and ourselves. Holding and receiving
words. Then, Bill stood.

Bill is tall and raw. He calls himself the cowboy writer.
and he is angry, very angry, with the brown men.
He blames his anger on these men, though he names no names.

Men who stole his job.
Not his job exactly, metaphorical job, the job of his friends.
Spittle flies as he talks.

I look at the spray under the pretty lights of the tent.
The cowboy writer works downtown in an office
with tall windows and thick upholstered chairs.

He was poor, he tells us, eyeing me pointedly, I squirm,
my chair digs into my old worn pelvis. I listen politely,
anything else might give credence to his testimony.

He yells, "White privilege, my ass. I was poor as mice."
The vein at his temple bulges, his calloused hands tremble.
I want to soothe his pain.

It is a funny thing
this unfounded
empathy, though I was never poor,

unlike the story he expects me to have, I know.
I want to say, See, Bill, I wore these pearls and nice clothes,
and yet suspicion follows my accent.

"It is not fair, you bleeding hearts, I worked all my life." His fist
beats his chest, as if this act makes it
a mea culpa.

I have worked too,
yet my olive skin sticks to me,
like the police: "Why are you running?"

Bill pounds one hand in the other and looks startled,
"I have worked with them, the brown men, nice fellows, mind me,
I am no racist."

The chair is colder or maybe tonight is darker,
Bill, I say again in my head, Billy Boy, it is not the money.
As you talk, I look at your stained

shoes, workman shoes, white man shoes.
Again, I wish I could be frank, but then—
I would be the typical, hysterical, angry Latina.

Still I remember
the way you left the table at noon today
throwing your napkin, your food untouched

when I began to speak Spanish
to a young girl,
a Latina,
she was a poet.

A White Child in the *New* América

Dimples rest at the base
of each callus-free finger.

They are as white as a dandelion's seed
but my weathered olive paw swallows them whole.

Hand in hand, we cross the street,
his—a total trust.

A speeding car flies by too close
His trust, my folly—yet he laughs.

We look at treats as we pass
strolling slowly at his pace.

Time has not limited his hunger.
He wants everything he sees—

His wants, my fears.

A blue butterfly lands on a dirty wall,
maybe an omen, for now just an insect.

We watch it open and close its wings,
they remind me of his eyelids.

Suddenly, it flies away
just like this child's dreams.

Rain

(Beautiful Outlaw Poem)

When clouds zag in this boxful sky, laden with liquid, I walk back
    to see you in the clown pajamas I fixed. Back when I was still
    the queen you loved. Unblemished and magical.

You were six. Me, the powerful conqueror of evil. I schooled
    myself, juggling love with sickness.
But I wilted in your doting eyes. No longer the *'bestest'* of
    mommies. No longer idolized.

Here was cancer's open entrance, a shadow formed a vortex
    between your trust
and zeal. No longer queen. Gone the free play keen on joy and mud
    adventures.

You were too small to realize that lovely magic is limited. Justice
    is frail. A bubble as the quiet stories ripped by disease,
    something I, your mother, was powerless to fix.

I Went to Mona Island
When I Was Sixteen and

it was raining, so I turned on
the TV.

New foil on the antennas,
still needed to be rearranged.

Finally! A channel—
National Geographic.

I grabbed my big bamboo needles
and sat on the old fat chair,

the arm rest had a new hole,
soon it will need to be reupholstered

The skein label said
Mango Delight.

Indeed, the color and the name
made me hungry.

TV on mute
I cast 143 stitches

Something—
an image in black and white,

caught my attention.
I faltered in my count.

There!

The xeric landscape,
of sand and iguanas,

I wondered—
then it happened,

a girl in the background.
I ran to the TV to still the image

but I was a minute late.
She was no longer at the center,

frozen and out of focus.
You could still see an unblemished leg,

the cincher
her knitted shirt.

My fifteen-year-old found me
still as a statue, holding my mango delight

standing so close
my nose almost touched the flat screen.

"Whatcha doing?"
in that irritating slang

biting into a Fuji apple.

I knew the apple would be discarded—
half eaten.

"Mihija," I said placing my index finger on the screen,
"I think...that's me."

But she took a loud bite
of her crisp apple

so she shrugged her shoulders,
and left me

alone
with the frozen image.

Ostracon From Those Years

You walked barefoot by the playground
dressed ablaze in rage.

Astoria had too high a bridge,
the ambulance seemed too small a place.

Your water bottle was filled with vodka
you fell making the bed.

The dog never fed,
the grass dead.

Ten hours in the ER waiting,
you laughed as I shared my fears.

The running shoes without laces laid
next to the cascading trophies out the window.

These etched the stone from those years.

The Poem She Wrote Without Writing

was peeling her skin to find termites

borrowing deep, tracing the flow of nerves.
It was her lecture on immobility

for years of perceived abuse,
waves that stilled her breath.

She cursed me then,

a foul language that betrayed her beauty.
Those words, a paintbrush

of an unknown landscape,
waged a war in that narrow ambulance,

an inward desert filled with rotten teeth.
A desire to bring her back

radiant like in the beginning when
the word became flesh.

The World Cup is Too Full

and life should be a football game
us versus an open green field—

rules all set.

Screams from fans
not children torn

from mother's arms at a border.
Look from the moon, where is the border?

The furor of heartbeats set upon a goal
not of the explosives that tore the neighborhood.

The smell of rockets overhead
the blues, the reds, just lines

of colorful smoke that adhere to flags.
Lines in single file cross the turnstile

and youngsters with hands over their heads.
An alien might confuse the two for the same.

The suffocating loudness of crowds,
dust, and blood-stones.

Even the power of seeing the abandoned shoe
among the detritus, the skeleton

of a horse covered in lime,
camouflaged and lost in all the painted,

covered,
and torn faces

made for this moment—
rules all set.

Recipe for a Crystal Nation

Let's smash all our dishes,
glasses too. Then, the bottles—

and any crystal.
Let's ransack our neighbors' dishes

and the glass of distant foes.
Save a bottle of red wine—

Place all the broken shards
and make a crystal city,

let it scratch its way to a cloud.
Wait for a sunny, smog-free day

and watch the prisms form,
light's balancing act

that signals the time
to open the bottle

and pour yourself a glass.

III

Between the Legacies of Memory
—because there is always
a beginning to the eye of the lizard

.

Sublimation From Neglect

I'm forgetting words
native words,

first language words,
words filled with mother's milk.

They left without notice.
Sin adios,

after all a is to and dios
is god.

One day they stood,

and disappeared like this morning's fog,
thick and eloquent like soup,

so quickly insubstantial I wonder
if I dreamt the fog—the words.

Simple words like hum and antimony,
what made me think of them?

Their absence?
I want the need for their song.

waves from the inner passage

(Pantoum poem)

no more heroes in this landscape
just the quiet repose of ocean
burnishing with exquisite foam
but lacking the sound of waves

just the quiet repose of ocean
hidden beneath discarded sand
but lacking the sound of waves
and all the shells that came to rest

hidden beneath discarded sand
each grain captures a passing thought
and all the shells that came to rest
in these shores so far away from land

each grain captures a passing thought
burnishing with exquisite foam
in these shores so far away from land
no more heroes in this landscape

For *Passiflora edulis*

(Pantoum poem)

In my father's garden a wild vine grew,
lush and verdant and full of passion fruit.
His uncertain hands pruned this precious vine
for her fecundity, he knew, was filled with sun.

Lush and verdant and full of passion fruit,
the taste of laughter in every nibble
for her fecundity he knew was filled with sun,
the memory of this man who loved his soil.

The taste of laughter in every nibble
la Parcha Verde or Granadilla
the memory of this man who loved his soil,
in those years of rain, anguish, and sometimes love.

La Parcha Verde or Granadilla,
his uncertain hands pruned this precious vine
in those years of rain, anguish, and sometimes love.
In my father's garden a wild vine grew.

Hiraeth From an Oregon Beach to a Lost Island

(Ghazal poem)

I return to the image of a sky that devoured an ocean,
and an ocean that splits my ghosts from the living.

Not by cloud or breath can I touch those faces,
faded along with their voices, a choice I made for living.

Their memories crowded, too much noise and too many soft touches,
shattered echoes that bounce on waves no longer full of living.

Even the violent whitecaps, as brief as a wet eyelash,
eventually disappear in a blink, but leave an imprint on the living.

Maybe it is the cold sand under my feet, a cruel reminder
of rooms filled with jovial conversations fit for living.

How many shades of blue are needed to fill a landscape?
How many waves can drown the sound of the un-living?

A cold breeze that hints of fog clashes with an imaginary trade wind,
viento alisio, heat discarded like gossamer through the travels of
    the living.

An Oregon beach where palm trees are made with sand and wishes
and allure from rocks that jut over the surface, exposing the frailty
    of living.

Where in the vastness of sand, heat, and ego do shades of people go?
Each grain forgotten, bleached, if not for the remembrances of
    the living.

My father's soft gentle hand, my uncle's unbearable guitar, En mi
   Viejo San Juan
floating on these distant waters away from the island alone and
   un-living.

Even the names shimmer, Asunción, Amelia, Esperanza, floating
   like plankton
on ocean waves awaiting sounds to be whispered, shouted, from
   those still living.

What I Left Behind:

The singing coquí that says it is six o' clock
sending the cattle egrets to roost.

El machetero walking barefoot
with his machete on his painful gleaming back.

Aunts and uncles and their lecture on propriety
mothers calling from balconies, a sandal ready at hand.

Suppers full of achiote, recaito, recipes untold
arroz con pollo y tembleque.

Nuns with rulers and tight wimples
the Cathedral, Dulce Nombre de Jesús.

The eternal beggars and gypsies
that will have your money for a blessing.

Brown and black boys stripped to khaki pants
held with a rope of hope, shouting—*Chiclets!*

La Victoria, Woolworth and La Central
with its aroma of roasted coffee at siesta time.

Tiered servants in aprons
and the debutantes.

Chandeliers, handmade lace and dances on Sunday afternoons
and, of course, the horseraces at El Comandante.

Traffic jams, the heat and humidity
of stolen kisses behind a neighbor's yard.

Sex on open sand with turquoise waters
darkened skies, where walls are missing.

The whistling duck and the Antillean grackle
with its knowing yellow eye.

Lizards caught with a slim blade of grass
the feel of a father's hand.

The gallant Plaza, the busy streets at night
the illusion of grandeur, the pride.

Guayabas full of worms
piraguas full of dreams.

The bitterness of a tamarindo stolen
just for the hint of sun.

Earthquakes and hurricanes
drives on twisted roads.

El Morro fortress with its thick walls
that can't detain the exodus.

What did I leave behind?
Almost nothing at all.

At Midnight's Turn

to find that hair no longer shines.
Creases at the side of the temple

gone gray.
Children's laughter

no longer fills hallways.
No sidestepping

over bodies at play
on dirty carpets,

beds always made.
Their departure rids

relentless-exhausting noise,
a deafening silence remains.

Empty arms that
support no weight.

Loggerheads and Leatherbacks

(Cebú poem)

Once in the Caribbean brine,
away from the prying eyes of my father,
lost in blue with the smell of fish-bones on our skin
I gave myself to you, soft as the inside of a mollusk.

Bashful as the turtles we were chasing,
coast after coast following the nesting sites,
every egg marked and mapped,
each freckle traced by your finger—naming constellations.

We navigated with the laughter of our crew,
two desperate boys, who robbed at night
the future of those nests, unseen to us 'the protectors'
while we stole each other's breath under the *Antinous* stars.

Plundered nests before the sun entered those waters,
under the fading eye of Yucayú,
just as you left without saying adiós,
leaving me alone with sand, ocean, and newly discovered fire.

Sisal, USA

This tapestry of fibers,
thread by thread,
a modern experiment—
of shuttle across the shed—
                    assimilate, assimilate.
Leaving textures felted,
buttressed
against one another.
A smattering of colors
where weft and warp sing
discordant,
at times communal.
New, abundant,
like nowhere else
on earth.
This spinneret of languages and tastes.

Turn the fabric!
Inside, the colors invert.
Esthetic of sheer absorbency,

barrios, nachbarschaft, hayi, fujin, xaafad ...home

expand, interlock
a new gauge.
Like cotton in the beginning
holds the weight,
the cross grain,
the strength
in the pain of its remembrance,
but should stand in its rightful place
        center.

Yet, this older generation calls to halt the new fabric—
                    Assimilate! Assimilate!
As if burlap could ever outworth silk.
The dyes in this tapestry are not a stamp.

The colors live in the breadth
that has no selvage.

We Blamed the Catholic Nuns

for their black and white wimples
distorted young faces.

Sister Catherine Agnes ruler in hand,
"Orientals, so called for the cartographers of old
 that oriented the world with their lovely maps;
the first maps."

So we drew maps of The Island
on paper plates,

made bonsais from pipe cleaners,
construction paper.

So many perished under that rule of hers
—the communist Chilean poet
—the blaspheming novelist of Colombia.

They never lived in the classroom.
"If I ever see any of you reading that filth!"

We could see the ruler landing
with a loud slap of flat wood on flesh.

But the communist and the blasphemer
we read

under the mango tree
near the unused tennis court.

Sweet stolen moments during recess,
allured by the intoxicating alliance of a friend.

Uniforms irreversibly soiled
by red alluvium.

A List of What I Learned in Kindergarten:

Buster Brown shoes are ugly
and eat the back of your socks.

If you get a stain on your uniform
you get the wooden paddle.

Other kids are very gullible; I told them I have a friend
in my backpack, and they believed me!

Sultana crackers and orange juice
don't go well together. (Taste like puke.)

Mrs. Manzanero is stupid
she sings no-sense songs.

My cousin tells me I am stupid,
Mrs. Manzanero is teaching English songs.

My desk is the messiest in the room
and the teacher doesn't smell like apples, like her name.

Lizards hang by the window, but if one gets on top of another
and you watch, they send you to Mother Superior's office.

Little girls cry on the first day of kindergarten
and I wonder why.

My uncle says it is because they miss their mothers
and I wonder then what that would be like.

El Morivivi—*Mimosa pudiente*

She knows me not as shy
but as her friend.

This inevitable tendency
to close my leaves.

Everyday she comes to play
or pull my flowers.

I can feel the earthquake of her laughter
the tender pressure of her touch.

Obligingly, I close my leaves
and she waits for them to open.

It is a paused thoughtful conversation,
touch-close-open, air to green.

A warm breath of loneliness,
laughter, and childhood sorrow.

In time she will forget me, but for now
I turn my leaves to sun, and rain, and her.

On the Cathedral's Long Stairs
We Sidestepped the Invisible

Ursula, the gypsy,
had big green eyes

and elephantiasis
(We urged each other to poke her deformed leg)
She begged closest to the heavy wooden doors.

José, our favorite beggar,
born without eyes,

his eyelids transparent
like the shed skin of a garbanzo bean

finely bordered with millipede lashes
caked in suppurating phlegm.

He knew, by sound,
what coin we gave him

as it fell
into his cup.

Puerto Rican Krummholz

On the very top of El Yunque
there are trees, twisted, thickened

by the daily burden of living,
tall as a Mayan woman.

Just as labored by constant clouds
of rain and wind and wish.

Bromeliads and ferns sprout
from every crevice of their dwarf trunks.

Colorful gowns that adorn their bark
break the monotony of green and toil.

The tropical breeze here births cold
leaves covered in ocellated droplets.

Fairy jewels hidden in occult anoles
and the eye of Yúcahu.

Self-Portrait

I rained from memory
a still life—a painting.

Dipped in a brush
of biology's colors,

Frida then Oller.
Both worlds of castanets,

knitted mantillas,
and hands in circled sand.

Where rosaries and crucifixes
burn the lips of sinners.

Surrounded by water currents
salted by the high mesa.

Altiplano to Cordillera
full of sun and loneliness.

Beautiful Rebellion

If I am a weed, the alien
to be plucked

out of this garden,
forced to be manicured,

I say,
not today.

Today
I am surrounded by the buzz

of honeybees,
and sunlight bites my thighs

as a playful lover could.
Let's meet

in the center green
where so much beauty grows;

surrender your shears
share with me this blush...

Things I Thank:

silence of the open space
filled with the sounds of grace

words that float like feathers
from a peacock's tail

a flower moved by breeze
freedom of unshackled stillness

the invitation of a brilliant petal
a visit by a thirsty bee

that doe who let me watch the birth of her fawns
on my meadow, the grass that raised to meet them

a ray of sun to an open seed above cement
two cotyledons of green a certain future hope

honeysuckle in my neighbor's garden
fills her with an unexpected joy

onions and garlic in my dancing hand
my greedy knife to meet them

a long descent from a mountain top
reward at the end of a climb

waiting patiently to hold this child
a lifetime of stories real and imagined

at the beach the child gazes inside a tide pool
full with anemones, starfish, and liquid wonder

abundance of our home's lonely travel
around the sun is our gift and gratitude

each stone along this path
journey with sight and breath

have a name for all the shells and clouds
and carry them baskets

Nightcap

Before indigo, there is the darkness
that spans half a lifetime.

Open to stars and scintillating voices
that reverberate through sleek landscapes

barren of shapes but figures are made—
phosphorescent like memories.

Aggregates of time spent near campfires
that send red shooting sparkles

towards the heavens,
and heavens that scurry to engulf them.

Acknowledgments

First and foremost, I would like to thank the members of the Grand Ronde Writers, Blue Mountain Writers, and Salem Poetry Writers for their invaluable support and critique through these years. Thank you also to the staff and students of the Eastern Oregon University MFA program who are working each day to bring the written word to move and make change. To all the editors of journals and magazines where some of these poems have appeared in different earlier forms. And to my family whose lives give meaning to mine.

My deepest gratitude to all the editors who have published earlier versions of these poems.

"*Larix larcina*, not a Slag" *Cirque Journal*, #23 Vol 12, 2021

"The Seven Poles at Minam/Circled Chief Joseph Dreams" *Cirque Journal*, #23 Vol 12, 2021

"The Road Curves" *Terra Incognita*, anthology, *Bob Hill Publishing*, 2019

"Crossing the Border to Aztlan" *Terra Incognita*, anthology, *Bob Hill Publishing*, 2019

"Ruckle Road Quarantine" */pãn/dé/mïk/ An Anthology of Pandemic Poems by OPA Members*, 2020

"A White Child in the *New* América" *Terra Incognita*, anthology, *Bob Hill Publishing*

"The World Cup is Full" *Terra Incognita*, anthology, *Bob Hill Publishing*, 2019

"Waves From the Inner Passage" *Grand Little Things*, August, 2022

"Pantoum for Passion Fruit" *Grand Little Things*, April, 2021

"Hiraeth From an Oregon Beach to a Lost Island" 3rd place for a Ghazal, *Oregon Poetry Association*, 2019

"Cebú Poem: Loggerheads and Leatherbacks" Poem, *Grand Little Things*, 2021

"Sisal, USA" *Oregon East Journal* Volume LI, 2020 Edition

"Beautiful Rebellion" Anvil Tongue Books, Anvil Tongue, July 2021

Also by Amelia Díaz Ettinger

These Hollowed Bones, Sea Crow Press (2024)

Self Dissection, Poetry Box (2023)

Fossils on a Red Flag, Finishing Line Press (2021)

Learning to Love a Western Sky, Airlie Press (2020)

Speaking at a Time / Hablando a la Vez, Redbat Books (2015)

About the Author

Amelia Díaz Ettinger is a bi-lingual poet and writer whose work spans poetry, fiction, and essays, often exploring themes of bicultural identity, language, displacement, and family. She is the author of *Learning to Love a Western Sky*, *Speaking at a Time / Hablando a la Vez*, and *These Hollowed Bones*, as well as the chapbooks *Fossils on a Red Flag* and *Self Dissection*. Her newest book, *Between*, continues her lyrical exploration of cultural inheritance, memory, and the spaces we navigate to find belonging.

Her poetry and prose have appeared in numerous literary journals and anthologies, and she has presented her work across the country. A 2025 recipient of the **Edna L. Holmes Fellowship for Young Adult Fiction** through Oregon Literary Arts, Díaz Ettinger lives in rural Oregon, where she writes, teaches, and tends to a small farm with her partner and too many pets.

www.ameliadíazettinger.com

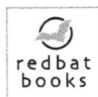

www.ingramcontent.com/pod-product-compliance
Lightning Source LLC
Chambersburg PA
CBHW030053100426
42734CB00038B/1556